THE
GOOD NEWS,
BAD NEWS
JOKE BOOK

by Jovial Bob Stine

Pictures by B. K. Taylor

*For Matty, who is Good News
even though he thinks my jokes
are Bad News*

Published by The Trumpet Club

666 Fifth Avenue, New York, New York 10103

Copyright © 1990 by R. L. Stine

ISBN: 0-440-84159-3

Printed in the United States of America
January 1990

10 9 8 7 6 5 4 3
OPM

OUR GUARANTEE TO YOU

This book was carefully laugh-tested by a team of well known scientists. The scientists were locked in an airtight room where they read the jokes to themselves and to each other 24 hours a day without stop.

Every single joke was tested. Any joke that did not get a huge laugh was thrown out.

Eventually, *all* of the jokes had to be thrown out.

Then, the scientists were thrown out.

As a result, we can guarantee that each and every joke in this book is 100 percent pure joke. There are no joke fillers or joke by-products.

Because of our careful testing, we can also guarantee that there are no misteeks anywhere in this boook.

The Good News: There aren't any more pages like this.

The Bad News: This is the best page in the book!

GOOD NEWS!
IT'S TIME FOR JOKES

It's Good News When
They serve pizza instead of liver in the lunchroom.

But It's Bad News When
The pizza tastes just like liver!

It's Good News When

At recess, the big kids on the playground ask you to join their basketball game.

But It's Bad News When

They want you to be the basketball.

It's Good News When

The most popular girl in school passes a note to you.

But It's Bad News When

The note asks if you can lend her five dollars.

It's Good News When

The teacher thinks your oral book report is the best one she's ever heard.

But It's Bad News When

She likes it so much, she makes you give it in front of the entire school!

It's Good News When

The dentist says your X-rays are perfect.

But It's Bad News When

Your X-rays are perfect but your teeth are a mess!

It's Good News When

The dentist takes one look at you and says, "I see you've been brushing at least twice a day."

But It's Bad News When

Then he says, "Enough about your hair. Now let's have a look at your teeth!"

It's Good News When

Your dad says you don't have to mow the lawn this afternoon.

But It's Bad News When

It's because you have to rake all the leaves first!

It's Good News When

Your dad says you can have any pet you want.

But It's Bad News When

He says it on April First, and then laughs really loud!

It's Good News When

Your parents say you won't ever have to clean your room again.

But It's Bad News When

It's because they gave your room to your sister!

It's Good News When
Your parents think you may have musical talent.

But It's Bad News When
To find out, they make you take violin lessons three times a week!

It's Good News When
Your mom says, "Okay, go ahead—you can eat your dessert before your dinner."

But It's Bad News When
The dessert today is lima beans!

It's Good News When
You don't have to watch your little sister all afternoon. You can do anything you want.

But It's Bad News When
They've asked your little sister to watch *you*!

THE VISIT

It's Good News When
Your favorite aunt has come for a visit.

But It's Bad News When
She's getting your room.

It's Good News When
That means you get to move in with your brother.

But It's Bad News When
Your brother snores and talks in his sleep.

It's Good News When
Your aunt brought you a present.

But It's Bad News When
It's the same baby toy she gave you five years ago!

It's Good News When
She didn't pinch your cheek real hard the way she always does.

But It's Bad News When
She pinched *both* cheeks!

It's Good News When
She said you look taller.

But It's Bad News When
She said taller than her poodle!

It's Good News When
She complimented you on your report card.

But It's Bad News When
The compliment was, "It's nice to see that you still have so much room for improvement!"

It's Good News When
She wants to take you out for a special dinner.

But It's Bad News When
It's a special all-peas dinner at a local vegetarian restaurant.

It's Good News When
After dinner she takes you to a movie.

But It's Bad News When
It's a documentary about vanishing wildlife in Banff!

It's Good News When
She tells her favorite funny stories about you.

But It's Bad News When
They're about how you took all your clothes off and did stupid things when you were little!

It's Good News When
Only two of your friends were over when she told the stories.

But It's Bad News When
They can't wait to tell everyone else in school!

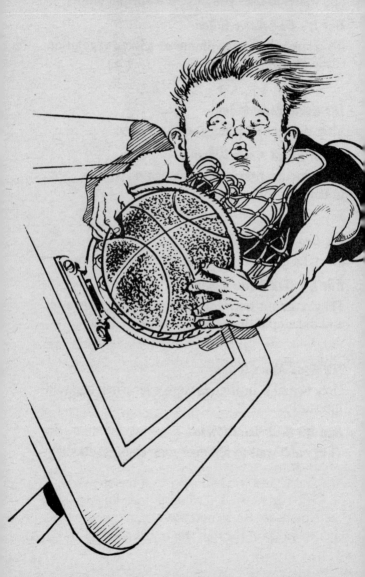

The crowd leaped to its feet and roared as the star of the basketball team dribbled down the court, jumped high over the defender, and executed a gravity-defying slam dunk.

As everyone continued to shout, the coach came running out onto the floor to congratulate his player. "Johnson," he called up to him, "I've got good news and bad news about that slam dunk. The good news is you just scored the winning two points."

"And what's the bad news?" Johnson asked.

"The bad news is it's gonna take us a while to get you down from there. Why can't you remember to let go of the ball when you shoot?"

*T*he baseball player wasn't known for his speed, but he decided to take a chance. Very few players in the history of the game had ever attempted to steal like this—but he just had a feeling he could do it.

Keeping his eyes on the pitcher, he took a deep breath and made his move. Before he even realized it, he was sliding, sliding toward the bag at top speed. YES! YES! His cleats hit the plate. He was safe!

As he got up and dusted himself off, the team's manager came out to congratulate him. "Wilson, I've got good news and bad news about that move," he said. "The good news is that was the greatest slide into home plate I've ever seen."

"And what's the bad news?" Wilson asked.

"The bad news is it really isn't necessary to slide when you're coming up to bat!"

The football player took the snap from center and moved forward quickly with three short steps. As he kicked, he heard a solid THUD, and he knew it was a good punt. He watched happily as it sailed up, up, out of the field and into the bleachers. It sailed at least 60 yards! he thought.

He turned around to see his coach running across the field to congratulate him. "Stanley," shouted the coach, "I've got good news and bad news about that kick. The good news is it was the longest kick I have ever seen."

"And what's the bad news?" Stanley asked.

"The bad news is you kicked your helmet—not the ball!"

17

GOOD NEWS
FROM PARENTS

1. "Your room is a mess! But I love it that way.
It reminds me of my room when I was your age!"

2. "That dog you made us buy for you barked and howled all night long. Gee, what a swell watchdog!"

3. "You want to invite a friend to sleep over? Wouldn't it be more fun if you invited five or six?"

4. "Please don't fill up on dinner. I don't want you to spoil your appetite for the chocolate layer cake!"

5. "The freezer's on the blink. Quick—finish all this ice cream before it melts!"

6. "A few mild aches and pains? You'd better stay home from school today."

7. "We ran out of cod cakes, so I guess I'll make pizza for dinner instead."

8. "All of your friends have that new Nintendo game? Well, then you should have it too!"

9. "I know this is hard on you, but we're going to have to move. We'll be moving to Beverly Hills."

10. "Gee, that's a great record. Could you play it louder so I can hear it too?"

11. "You're certainly on the phone a lot. Why don't we put one in your room?"

12. "Kids, I quit my job so I could go into business for myself. I'm going to open a video game arcade!"

MORE GOOD NEWS: THE JOKES CONTINUE!

It's Good News When

Your mom says it's okay for the dog to sleep in your bed.

But It's Bad News When

You never realized the dog snores!

It's Good News When

You're the only candidate to run for student government president.

But It's Bad News When

You still lose the election!

It's Good News When

You don't have to walk the dog in the rain.

But It's Bad News When

That's because it's snowing!

It's Good News When

You win first place in a contest.

But It's Bad News When

It's the Teenage Mutant Ninja Turtle Lookalike Contest!

It's Good News When

Your grandmother doesn't send another gray, woolly bathrobe for your birthday this year.

But It's Bad News When

She sends gray, woolly pajamas instead!

It's Good News When

Your best friend shares *everything* with you.

But It's Bad News When

Your best friend has a cold!

It's Good News When

On the day of your class picnic, the weather forecast calls for "fair and sunny."

But It's Bad News When

You're drenched by two inches of "fair and sunny" before noon!

It's Good News When

Your new babysitter loves to play video games.

But It's Bad News When

She loves to play them with her boyfriend while you watch!

It's Good News When

You're amazed to find that the shoe store actually has the style of sneakers you want in your size.

But It's Bad News When

"Bunny Ear Pink" wasn't exactly the color you had in mind!

It's Good News When

The most popular guy in school chooses to sit next to you in the lunchroom.

But It's Bad News When

All he wants is to tell you you've spilled spinach down the front of your blouse!

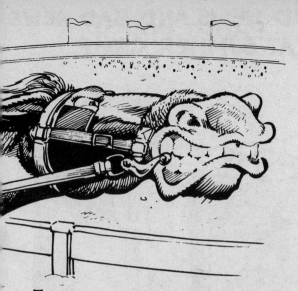

*T*he jockey held the reins tightly and leaned forward on his galloping horse. "Let's go, let's go, let's go!" he urged, shouting over the thunder of hoofbeats as the horses raced down the home-stretch.

He could see it was going to be a close race, so he went to the whip. He felt the horse jolt as he tapped its flank, and he sprang forward. The jockey knew he was flying now, flying past the rest of the pack, flying over the finish line.

As the jockey struggled to catch his breath, he saw the horse's owner hurrying over to congratulate him. "I've got good news and bad news about that race," the owner said. "The good news is you finished first!"

"And what's the bad news?" asked the jockey.

"The bad news is your horse finished 18th!"

GOOD NEWS AND BAD NEWS AT SUMMER CAMP

It's Good News When

For the first time, you get to sleep in the top bunk.

But It's Bad News When

You never realized how much you roll around in your sleep!

It's Good News When
The food in the mess hall is really improved.

But It's Bad News When
You still can't hack the crust off the chocolate pudding!

It's Good News When
The kids in your bunk aren't all wimps and nerds this year.

But It's Bad News When
They all wonder how *you* got into their bunk!

It's Good News When
There are no more leeches in the lake.

But It's Bad News When
The water is much too polluted for leeches to live in!

It's Good News When
You don't have to make stupid beaded belts in arts and crafts.

But It's Bad News When
You have to make stupid beaded potholders instead!

It's Good News When
The archery counselor points you out as a good example.

But It's Bad News When
It's as a good example of what happens to someone who steps in front of the targets!

It's Good News When
They've added computers and computer games to your camp.

But It's Bad News When
They haven't added electricity yet!

It's Good News When
It rains during your camp-out, but you don't mind because you're snug in a tent.

But It's Bad News When
The tent leaks.

It's Good News When
You don't care if the tent leaks because you're snug inside a sleeping bag.

But It's Bad News When
Guess what else leaks?

It's Good News When

The swimming coach says you're the best swimmer in your group.

But It's Bad News When

He says you're still not quite ready to take off the inner tube!

It's Good News When

There are no annoying pillow fights in your bunk this year!

But It's Bad News When

It's because they didn't give you pillows!

It's Good News When

Your counselor announces there will be no five-mile hike this summer.

But It's Bad News When

Instead, it'll be a five-mile *jog*!

It's Good News When

Your counselor remembered to bring dozens of hot dogs to cook over the campfire.

But It's Bad News When

He remembered the hot dogs but forgot the matches.

It's Good News When

Raw hot dogs don't taste so bad if you put a lot of mustard on them.

But It's Bad News When

He forgot the mustard too!

It's Good News When

The mosquitos aren't pestering you.

But It's Bad News When

They don't have a chance because of all the flies,
fleas, bees, spiders, and gnats!

GOOD NEWS
ABOUT HOMEWORK

1. "Class, I'm afraid I asked you to read all of the wrong chapters last night. That means you're so far ahead you won't have to read any more for two weeks."

2. "Oops. Time's up and I forgot to check the homework today. Oh well, just check over your own."

3. "Your homework for tonight is to go home and have fun. You've all been working much too hard!"

4. "I lost your book reports, so I'm going to have to give you all A's."

5. "You say your dog ate your homework? No one's ever given me that excuse before! I'm giving you an A for originality!"

6. "Some of you have complained that my homework assignments have been keeping you from watching TV at night, so I've decided to stop giving homework."

7. "I always mark down for neatness. If your paper is too neat and perfect, it means you didn't work hard enough on it!"

8. "Your assignment for this week is to develop your conversation skills. Each night you are to talk on the phone to your best friend for at least an hour!"

9. "You forgot your homework? Well, we all make mistakes. For instance, I forgot to write the test I was going to give you today!"

10. "I usually wouldn't accept a book report based on a Ninja Turtles comic book—but yours is so well written, I'll make an exception."

11. "Your science experiment for Monday is to study how eating massive amounts of chocolate bars and ice cream can affect your appetite."

JUST PLANE CRAZY

*T*he airline passengers were horrified when their plane began to bounce and jerk. Lunch trays slid off tray tables and suitcases fell from overhead compartments as the big plane lurched forward, then tilted sideways. The stewardesses were falling down in the aisles.

Suddenly two men in blue uniforms ran out of the cockpit, opened the emergency door, checked their parachutes, and then jumped out of the plane.

What's going on here? the passengers wondered.

A few minutes later, a stewardess made an announcement. "Ladies and gentlemen, I have bad news and good news," she said. "The bad news is that we have the worst pilot and copilot in the country. They both failed their pilot test, and they don't have a clue as to how to fly this plane."

"And what's the good news?" called a passenger.

"The good news is that it was them who just left!"

SPECIAL INTERMISSION PAGE!

Good News: You're only halfway through the book. Plenty more jokes to come!

Bad News: They're all just as bad as the ones you've already read!

THE FAMILY VACATION

It's Good News When
Your family is taking you on a two-week vacation.

But It's Bad News When
It's to the same leaky cabin by a lake you always go to.

It's Good News When
On sunny days, the lake is beautiful and perfect for swimming, sailing, and fishing.

But It's Bad News When
The forecast is for two weeks of rain!

It's Good News When
Your mom didn't forget your toothbrush this year.

But It's Bad News When
She forgot your whole suitcase!

It's Good News When
For once, you don't have to go to the bathroom the instant your dad backs the car down the drive.

But It's Bad News When
You have to go two blocks later!

It's Good News When
Mom and Dad don't have their usual fight about which is the best route to take.

But It's Bad News When
They're already not speaking to each other because they had that fight the night before!

It's Good News When
No flat tires this year!

But It's Bad News When
The engine died before any tire could go flat!

It's Good News When
Your summer allergies aren't bothering you.

But It's Bad News When
It's because you're much too carsick to be bothered by summer allergies!

It's Good News When
For once, you don't get into a shoving match in the back seat with your little brother.

But It's Bad News When
You get into a fist fight instead.

It's Good News When
Your dad doesn't get lost in the same place he always does.

But It's Bad News When
He gets lost in a *different* place.

It's Good News When

Your mom doesn't force you to sing 300 choruses of "The Bear Went Over the Mountain" to pass the time.

But It's Bad News When

Your little brother sings it anyway!

It's Good News When

You arrive at the campsite on time.

But It's Bad News When

No one cares. You're all too exhausted from the car ride to do anything!

It's Good News When

They made lots of improvements and really spiffed up the campsite during the winter.

But It's Bad News When

One of the improvements was tearing down your cabin!

3 FROM OUTER SPACE

A man was walking in the woods when he came upon a flying saucer. He went close to examine it. A door slid open and a huge alien monster climbed out. The monster stared down at the man with four eyes, his six arms all jiggling excitedly. The man didn't know whether to greet him or run for his life.

"I have good news and bad news for you," the monster said. "The good news is I've never met a human I didn't like."

The man smiled. "And what's the bad news?" he asked.

"The bad news is I like them boiled."

A man was walking along the beach when a flying saucer landed nearby. A door slid open and a gigantic alien monster stepped out onto the sand. The man stared at the monster, frozen in fear.

The monster stepped into the ocean, pulled out 55 huge fish one at a time, and gobbled them up. Then, licking his six lips, he walked up to the man.

"I have good news and bad news for you," the monster said. "The good news is I *never* eat between meals."

The man smiled and breathed a sigh of relief. "And what's the bad news?" he asked.

"The bad news is I've just had my appetizer. And now it's time for the main course!"

A man built himself a new house with everything in it shiny and new. He loved to work in the kitchen, which was the biggest and prettiest room in the whole house.

One day he found two hideous alien monsters from outer space in his kitchen. The monsters took one look at the man and started to argue loudly in a strange language. Then they started to fight. They clobbered each other with their enormous claws until one of the monsters fell to the kitchen floor and didn't move.

The victorious monster turned to the man and said, "I have good news for you. My friend and I just fought over who was going to eat you, and I won!"

"Why is that good news?!" cried the man.

"It's good news because he's a very messy eater and he would've just *ruined* this beautiful kitchen!"

GOOD NEWS FROM ALL OVER!

Ticket Seller

"The only seat I have left to the Bon Jovi concert is in the front row. Is that all right?"

Little Sister

"Why don't you choose what we watch on TV? You have better taste than me."

Teacher

"I know I just caught you passing this note in class. I just have one thing to say about it—your handwriting is really excellent!"

Violin Teacher

"I'm going to tell your parents that you really don't enjoy these lessons. I'm going to suggest that they buy you a stereo instead!"

Lunchroom Worker

"By mistake we received 12 crates of mozzarella cheese. So we'll have to serve nothing but pizza for at least two months!"

Stranger

"Is this your twenty-dollar bill?"

Little Brother

"I can see you and your friends would like some privacy. So I'll go up to my room and leave you alone."

Pizza Chef

"Here's your pizza. I let it cool for a while before I served it so you won't get third-degree burns from the first bite."

Movie Cashier

"You're right. This movie isn't worth four dollars. Here. I'll pay you two dollars to go in."

School Principal

"I'm sorry to have to announce this, but I have just learned that testing has been made illegal in this state."

TV Announcer

"Because of a special showing of Roger Rabbit cartoons, the President's address will not be seen tonight."

Gym Teacher

"So you're the one who threw that paper wad at me? You've got some throwing arm. I'd like you to be starting pitcher on the school baseball team!"

Doctor

"I'm sorry, but you really should put on 20 pounds."

Martian

"I have orders to bring an earthling to our Junk Food Palace. Will you come quietly, or do I have to use force?"

CHEERS!

*J*ulie was determined to make the cheerleading squad at her school. The other girls laughed at her. They said she was too tiny and her voice was too small. But Julie knew she could do it.

She made up cheers and practiced them in her back yard for weeks before the cheerleading tryouts. The neighbors all thought she was weird, but Julie didn't care. She wanted to be the best new cheerleader on the squad.

On the day of the cheerleading tryouts, Julie couldn't think of anything else. She was so nervous and excited! After school, she threw her books in her locker and headed to the tryout room.

She couldn't wait another moment. She knew she was good. And she was going to show everyone how good!

She burst into the room, shouted out a cheer, did two running cartwheels, leaped high in the air, did a back flip, and followed with a long clapping cheer at the top of her lungs, and two more flying cartwheels.

Mrs. Parker, a teacher, came running up to her. "Julie, I've got good news and bad news about your performance," she said. "The good news is that was the wildest, loudest, most enthusiastic cheerleading I've ever seen in my life!"

"And what's the bad news?" Julie asked.

"The bad news is the cheerleading tryouts are across the hall. This is the teachers' lounge!"

GOOD NEWS AND BAD NEWS ABOUT SHOPPING

It's Good News When

The dress you had your eye on is 50 percent off.

But It's Bad News When

The *dress* is 50 percent off—not the price!

It's Good News When

Your mom says you're old enough to pick out all your own clothes.

But It's Bad News When

Your dad says you're old enough to pay for them, too!

It's Good News When

The sales clerk says, "We're having a special two-for-one sale—buy one, get one free."

But It's Bad News When

You can't afford *one*!

It's Good News When

At a local clothing store, you run into that cute girl from school.

But It's Bad News When

Just as you say hi to her, your mom comes by carrying several packages of underwear and loudly asks, "Now what size are you—large or extra-large?"

It's Good News When

They have the dress you want in the right color and the right size and at the right price.

But It's Bad News When

You don't see it until *after* you've bought a non-returnable dress you don't like as well!

It's Good News When

You are amazed to see that the outfit you've wanted to buy is only $16.

But It's Bad News When

You were holding the price tag upside down.

It's Good News When

You buy the perfect Mother's Day present for your mom.

But It's Bad News When

She doesn't agree that a Nintendo game is the perfect Mother's Day present!

It's Good News When

Those new pre-shrunk jeans look great on you because you couldn't wear them any tighter.

But It's Bad News When

After one washing you discover the pre-shrunk jeans weren't pre-shrunk!

GOOD NEWS IN THE DENTIST'S OFFICE

1. "Braces? I don't believe in braces. I think crooked teeth give you more personality!"

2. "Your teeth are so strong and healthy, you can eat all the candy and sweets you like!"

3. "No, I don't have a drill. I don't believe in them."

4. "I'm sorry. The dentist has been called away on an emergency. Can we reschedule your appointment in about six months?"

5. "These X-rays show 12 cavities and serious gum disease. Oh—wait a minute. They're not your X-rays."

6. "If I hurt you in any way, you don't have to pay me."

7. "You're right. The fluoride treatment tastes disgusting. Let's just forget about it."

8. "I seem to have lost my Happy Tooth Chart. So I'm afraid I can't give you that lecture I always give on the correct way to brush your teeth."

9. "Come back in two or three years!"

A REAL DIVING SHOW

*T*he girl was so nervous before swimming class she didn't think she could leave the locker room. "I've never dived before," she told her best friend. "I just don't know if I can do it."

"What you should do is just run right out to the pool now and dive without thinking about it," her friend advised.

"Yes, I think you're right," the nervous girl agreed. So she hurried out of the locker room, ran across the pool, and as startled swimmers looked on, she stepped up onto the diving board, took a deep breath, and dived in.

When she surfaced, the swimming instructor was there to congratulate her. "I've got good news and bad news about that dive," she said. "The good news is it was a perfect jacknife."

"And what is the bad news?" asked the girl.

"The bad news is you should've put on your bathing suit before coming to the pool!"

It's Good News When

Your parents say they're getting you a bike that's better than any of your friends' bikes.

But It's Bad News When

Only your parents think that three wheels are better than two!

It's Good News When

Your mom says you can help yourself to all the ice cream you want.

But It's Bad News When

The only flavors in the freezer are Rhubarb Crunch and Anchovy Swirl.

It's Good News When

You think you got every single question on the history test right.

But It's Bad News When

That's what you thought the last time you flunked a history test!

It's Good News When

You're asked to try out for the soccer team.

But It's Bad News When

You're asked to try out for the soccer team—by the football team!

It's Good News When

Your parents double your allowance.

But It's Bad News When

Two times zero is still zero!

It's Good News When
Your parents say you can play your music as loud as you want.

But It's Bad News When
They add, "As long as you play it on an accordion!"

It's Good News When
The teacher postpones your arithmetic test.

But It's Bad News When
She postpones it to give you a surprise geography test!

It's Good News When
You finish the arithmetic test before everyone else.

But It's Bad News When
It's because you forgot to do the last four pages!

It's Good News When
For the first time in your life you get a haircut that you like.

But It's Bad News When
Everyone who sees you immediately asks, "What did you do to your hair?!"

It's Good News When

That boy you have a crush on finally notices you.

But It's Bad News When

He notices you because you sneezed and the gum came flying out of your mouth!

It's Good News When

This is the last joke. You've read the whole book!

But It's Bad News When

Now you have to think of some *other* way to waste your time!

ABOUT THE AUTHOR

JOVIAL BOB STINE has spent the past 102 years writing joke books for kids. Before that, he had a variety of jobs, including brick taster, rubber hat warmer, and professional dog tickler.

Some of his more popular joke book titles are *The Big Book of Unfunny Jokes*, *The Big Boy's First Book of Giggles*, *Jokes To Make You Cry*, *The Big Boy's First Book of Guffaws*, *World's Best Disease Jokes*, and *Jokes for While You Sleep*.

While he is well known for his many joke books, the author is perhaps most famous for the unusual things he does with live bait.

Mr. Stine lives in New York City with his keeper.

The unforgettable saga of a magnificent family

IN JOY AND IN SORROW

by JOAN JOSEPH

They were the wealthiest Jewish family in Portugal, masters of Europe's largest shipping empire. Forced to flee the scourge of the Inquisition that reduced their proud heritage to ashes, they crossed the ocean in a perilous voyage. Led by a courageous, beautiful woman, they would defy fate to seize a forbidden dream of love.

A Dell Book   **$3.50**   **(14367-5)**